The Eve of
CONCEPTION

The Eve of
CONCEPTION
Selections of Transition

DAVID WAYNE

J. Kenkade
PUBLISHING®
LITTLE ROCK, ARKANSAS

The Eve of Conception
Copyright © 2019 by David Wayne

J. Kenkade Publishing
6104 Forbing Rd Little Rock, AR 72209
www.jkenkadepublishing.com

J. Kenkade Publishing is a registered trademark.

Printed in the United States of America
ISBN 978-1-944486-85-3

This is a work of fiction. The views expressed in this book are those of the author and do not necessarily reflect the views of the publisher.

"THE JUNGLE CREED SAYS THE
STRONGEST FEED ON ANY PREY THAT
IT CAN
AND I WAS BRANDED A BEAST
AT EVERY FEAST
BEFORE I EVER BECAME A MAN."

(From the movie Deep Cover)

This book is dedicated to all of
those whispers that have never left my ears
spoken by my parents,
JD and Erma Jean White
God Bless

EVE
noun
The day or period of time immediately before
an event or occasion

CONCEPTION
noun
The action of conceiving a child or a
child being conceived

Introduction

The life that I have lived, thus far, can be characterized by one word. Ironic. Now at the middle age of forty four, I honestly can look back a say, "There are many things that I have said, that I wouldn't do, as a younger man, took happening in the opposite way to what was expected." There were many words and phrases spoken by my mother and father in the dusk of my adulthood I didn't understand. Now that the period of time between midnight and noon has come, those words from my parents are now more clearly understood. Loosing close friends to violence and family to the wrath of life has become all so familiar. Drug and crime addiction invited more problems to the attitude of thinking that I was grown. Boy I wish I could go back home. How I wish I could see my mother and father again. Please take me back to the days when I was in high school. There are so many things that I would do differently. The feeling of thinking it was too late takes me back to some of those old phrases like:

"Only the strong survive"
"There's no reward without a struggle"
"Just keep on living"
Yeah, *"Nothing comes to a sleeper but a dream"*

Throughout my life I have bear witness to many transgressions, iniquities, and pain applied by me. But I'm still here by the grace and mercy of God Almighty. I vow here and today that if I am blessed to see as many days tomorrow as I have yesterday, I will do things better and touch some lives and pass my blessings on. The followings compositions comprise words of my witness that inspired me to write. I hope you are inspired as the reader. The stories of a new birth. The days before and beyond. This is "The Eve of Conception".

Prosody

Books from paper
Pencils from sticks
The beauty of the tree
Brings the mind to this
Plant seed to earth
And water to grow
Follow under the Son
Now true strength is shown
Letters to syllables
Syllables to words
With that one perfect union
Poetry is heard

The construction of syntax
The power of speech
From the root to the leaf
Like a branch I reach
Knowledge is the key
A subtle get and give
Although it's leaves may fall

They sprout again next year
Trees produce, o, so many things
Like the utensils need
And the words being spoken
In this prosody

Doing Me

No complaints thus far
Better yet none worth mentioning
Sad songs never settled with me
Don't waste my time if there's
nothing good for you to say
A compliment is something that
always comes free
It don't cost a dime
For you to stay out of mine
Everything's going fine by me
See I'm just doing time
And can't wait to get home
And I refuse to let the time do me

Spirits

What a wonderful feeling a sober
mind possess
No more distraction to the
thought the thought process
So pain and grief I consume the
less
Good conscience decisions
promote low stress

One step at a time I walk today
Although it's rugged I make my
way
Through times of struggle I kneel
and prey
For all my strength comes from a
longing faith
I remember the words my father
used to say,
"A sober tongue speaks a wise
mind"

Too Late

It's too late to turn back now
Everything is now in place
No more broken promises
I'm protected by his grace
It's too late to turn back now
No more empty space
The table is set
No more regrets
For accepting now I'm saved

So I say goodbye to times of old
Farewell to yesterday
I'm dressed, prepared
To meet the one
Who sends his warm embrace
It's too late to turn back now
A brand new road is paved
So now I travel hand and hand
Led by his bright sunrays

Time

Time waits for no one
I have often heard one say
If time could wait I would not be
late
For class early today
When I rush time
I'm sure to find some things lost
on the way
On borrowed time
I come to find some things seem
out of place
When I waste time I fall behind
Deadlines
Appointments break
For time waits for no one
Today
Not yesterday

Faith

In the midst of darkness
Hands extended
Struggling to find my way
A small voice insists that I kneel
down and pray
Forgive me for my sins
Although I've gone astray
Help me to overcome those
obstacles
That block my right of way

I hear, believe, confess, repent
I have been baptized today
But I still wonder if the Lord is
pleased enough
To let me in the gate
I'm weakened by a life of sin
Dear Lord I will obey
Restore my soul
Please help me hold
Onto everlasting faith

Journey

I am power
I am wisdom
I am knowledge and
understanding
I am an old soul
Therefore my spirit overwhelms
within me
So deep
I am young and growing and
faithful

Follow my instruments
I am peaceful
Full of love and joy
I struggle to prepare myself
For the blessings I know to come
I am strong and wise and yet so
tired
I can't change the things I know
But I can change the things I sew

Therefore we live, learn, and grow
So the ones after us will know
Be mindful in our journey
Don't let mindless things
discourage us
For grace is our destiny

("Robert Simmons")
(N.O)

If I Knew Then

If I knew then what I know now
So much more I would achieve
So much time I could have saved
So many things you wouldn't
believe
If I knew then what I know now
I wouldn't have lost my way
I would have took my precious
time
I would have listen to what father
said

If I knew then what I know now
I wouldn't have ever put blame on
you
I would have made better
decisions
Never would I've been made the
fool
If I knew then what I know now
I say these words so true

There would be less shame on me
And a lot more shame on you

From Sight to Song

Words take the place of pictures
Pictures take the place of words
They share a special bond
Like night to moon and day to
sun

Without pictures we lack the
sight
Without words we have no
tongue
Without the two we lack
something called soul
The main ingredient to a song

Without song where would we be
I wouldn't want to see
Because music is universal
Connecting land with the sea
How else could we relate?
Communicate with one another?

With pictures, words, soul, and
song
We make music with each other

Hello

Like the world takes its' turns
Life takes them too
Many degrees in a spin
Only to come back to you
For the seasons may change
Wind blows whispers untrue
We must stand upon faith
For our season is due
Now the cost may seem great
No more valuable than you
So many streams of good fortune
Which we long to find truth
Without you there's no me
Without me there's no you
I know the road has been rough
But the light sees us through
Though there's pain in deception
My heart stands unto you
Let's say goodbye to the old
And hello to the new

Seasons

As the raindrops tap the window
seal
Silence clears my mind
The gloom of morning lets the
day reveal
While yesterday is left behind
A cool gentle breeze shows fall is
here
Winter's not far behind

Golden leaves shed trees from
yesteryear
All fruit drop from the vine
Now mother natures' point is clear
We reach to father time
Crisp words of wisdom enter my
ear

The sound is sweet divine
With song birds' melody to hear
The spring's not hard to find

As flowers bloom, we persevere
Blessed to be one of mankind
The sun of summer wipes away
the tear
Drop stains we left behind
I am blessed today I am still here
The change is truly mine

Minus the Fear

Now adversity is never asleep
Stand tall and stay on focus
You may not get a second chance
If you don't take the notice
No reward without a struggle
A never ending fight
Live for today
Or die here tonight
There may not be tomorrow
Reparation's due
Give it to me now
I cannot stand to lose
Too much is on the plate
There's way too much at stake
Family is in my corner
So I bulldoze the way
I don't care what people say
Stay in control by faith
Keep your eye on the prize
That's what mother used to say

And when all the smoke is clear
I will be standing here
With another Victory
Minus the fear

Tomorrow

Subtle whispers of hope dry the
tear stained pillow
The same way as the sun dries
raindrops from the window
Though it seems to be distant
I hold faith close to the heart
Anxiously trying to fit pieces
From a life torn apart
So many things of the norm
Are now called memories
I pray and hope when it's my time
The creator remembers me
Weighing the good with the bad
Putting my heart on trial
Take in account of the road
That I have walked since a child
Count the many lives I have
touched
Separate the smiles from frowns
For I have walked through the
valley

Like death was nowhere to be
found
Please heal the wounds on my feet
Blood drops from broken glass
Shine the light on the future

And let the past be past
Shine the light on the future
I have found the way at last
No more looking backwards
Put to sleep all that's bad
Awaken into a new day
And blessed behold a new way
Where yesterday is history
And tomorrow is meant to be for
you and me

Eyes on the Sun

Today is the day I call my own
My eyes are on the sun
So much to do
I lace my shoes
I have had my share of fun
No time to play
Be on my way
Until the day is done
I set my goals
Let all else go
And fight until it's won
Pursue the task at hand I see
Success is drawing close
I knock three times
If all else fails
I'm knocking down the door
And in my destiny
I lean towards the possibility
To gain more speed
No disbelief

Ever becomes of me
Refuse to lose
They come in twos
The victor's always one
Today's the day I call my own
My eyes are on the sun

Answer This

What goes wrong when questions
remain?
Is it the lack of research minds
strain to explain?

Gazing out of the window
Set on personal gain
Looking left
Leaving right
In the air to hang

A one-sided perception
One-eyed broken mirrors
Generation gap too large
So many won't come near us
Maybe we speak too low
The reason they don't hear us
Or do we talk too loud
The reason they fear us
Why can't we just raise hands like
in the classroom?

Without our classmates laughing
We need support from them too
Why does dad keep laughing?
We need support from him too
Why does mom keep laughing?
We need support from her too

What goes wrong when questions
remain?
Is it the wrong questions
That we ask once again?
Is there too little time for
someone to explain?

Or the desire to withhold all
information obtained
There's way too many people on
computer mainframes
And not enough entering libraries
A shortage on books really seems
scary
When questions remain

One Promise

Hollowed hearts of men scared by
the wages of sin
On the hunt to satisfy their
hungry bleeding souls
Without strategy they prey falling
victims to prey
Loss of direction not knowing
which way to go

Turning left at the sign, signaling
right, that's not right
Seeking light in the dark where
there's no light to be found
For their minds hold the key to
10,000 locks by the tongue
In a land where the natives don't
know if it's flat or round

And where moving too fast seem
to miss targets of interest
Shifting the axis of destiny

narrowing the lanes of ambition
In this land there's five seasons:
winter, spring, summer, and fall
Without repentance due season
brings doom to us all
Counting steps with precision
with one eye in the rear
Holding steadfast with dreams of
paradise in the clear
There's no books for the questions
Answers are all in the mirror
Low octane on confidence
motives fueled by fear
Watering seeds with
misconceptions
Weakening tomorrow
Looking forward, moving
backwards
Bandaging past wounds with
sorrow

Holding the limbs from broken
trees are all that's left of home
Fighting with sisters
Now blind in the wilderness left
to roam
Without a sword or shield, no

food just alone
With only one true possession
That's the promise
That one day I will be gone

You, Me, and We

Where are you going me?
Why not just stay at home?
There's so much for you to do
right here
But yet and still we go
At night I always pray for you
And keep your bible close
The closer I seem to get to you
The farther away we roam
When I have money I give it to
you
You act as if we don't
Most of your friends are not our
friends
When we need them they are
gone
I called you yesterday
You didn't pick up the phone
Did you change your number?
Or just not answer

We really would like to know
Where are you going me?
You left me here alone
I thought we were friends until
the end
You, me, and we
The perfect bond

A Second Look

Like a stone I cannot be moved
I remain on solid ground
If you take a second look
You will see I'm still around
My strength is what defines me
My goal is to never break
Never look down on what's
beneath
Being a cornerstone is in my fate
Gathered with mortar I construct
with structure
Piece the puzzle, connect the dots
Focus my mind on where I'm
going
Never worry about where I'm not
Keep my eyes upon the sun
What I surpass is left behind
Destinations far and beyond
Just seek and ye shall find
Like a stone I cannot be moved

I remain on solid ground
If you take a second look
You will see I'm still around

Let's Get Some Understanding

In this world of stone walls
Tall ceilings and long halls
Where two ears say they are
listening
But hear nothing at all
Where the tongue is the only
prisoner
Behind the bars of two lips
Seeking freedom in subtle
whispers
Hiding words behind the kiss
You see a dream is only a dream
Until the dreamer awakens
Thus far a chance is only a chance
Until someone takes it
Embracing thoughts from the
core
Are without life if unheard
It's unhealthy to withhold
pressure
Without a passageway to disperse

Lyrics, songs, keynotes, quotes
Riddles, rhymes, or chorus lines
Confessions before the judge
Speak the truth in back spines
Let us unwind
Words intertwined
Looking for truth
There's no use
For the line of understanding
Draws between me and you

Devil's Thorn

Hot days and cold nights
Without a way to the cure
The thickness of the wilderness
Is becoming hard to endure
No passage leads the way
The falcon stays on alarm
As the midst of Fogs Creek
Opens up Devils Thorn
No sign of life is left
All is due come to past
Through the windows of faith
Repair the broken hour glass
A small light shines from the sun
The glow comes from deep within
All that creeps and crawls
Entangled in web
At the pass of no end
In the mouth of Devils Thorn
Tall grass paves the way
Without the stories of old

There is no need for today
As the sun vanishes beyond
The moon reappears
From the shallows
Armed with shadows
Promising a new day is near

Love Jones

Here lies a very thin line between
love and addiction
A costly routine and subtle dance
with affliction
Holding hands with a substance
in which substance is missing
Broken hearts and torn lives from
unconscious decisions
Footprints left in lust, wondering
where went the love
Waking up from a coma,
wondering what happened to us

So many lies, blindfolds, and
words that cut like a knife
Powder residue on saucers and
empty bottles from last night
Stale smell from cigarette smoke,
empty packs
Still I search
Through waste baskets and ash
trays

No money, thinking,
I guess it could be worst
Escaping death, constantly
praying,
Begging the Lord for mercy
Late nights on long flights are
catching up in a hurry
Pillow soaked from cold sweats

So I search for the cure
At the tip of car keys
This life is becoming hard to
endure
Cut straws and pinky nails seem
to bloody my nose
Though I was raised in a good
home
I live where anything goes
Thought I was raised in a good
home
I live where anything goes
About to explode at any moment
like a can of C-4
Destined beyond the stars
Dodging the comets in darkness
Think twice before choosing
Look both ways before crossing

Look Away

Saturday, Saturday
Another day away
All praises to the one above
So I kneel down to pray
As I sit alone this eight by ten
Seems larger here today
Among the wilted seeds of the
land
But still I hold my faith
Conveyed by grace
I cleanse my space
My travel's underway
With head up high no wonder
why
My confidence is gained
And for beyond a harden soul
The scale has tilt away
I gaze for in the distance
Victory has come in play
My destiny is clear now

For me this present day
My eyes are set in front of me
What's left behind
I look away

Lonely Traveler

I set my travels from land
In the valley below
With my mind upon the
mountain top
Peak white as snow
Though the image seems near
I have so far to go

For my baggage is heavy
Still my burdens are low
See, my journey's upon faith
That's why I speak eyes closed

To my father who listens
And points direction to go
Dusty trails, shallow streams
I even part grassy knolls
Whatever it takes for me to get
there
It is with victory shown
Steep cliffs as I elevate

So the body stays close
To his word to prevent falling
To what's left below
I am lifted by his grace
Therefore salvation is close
What a site for sore eyes
As I slowly approach

It is with goodness and mercy
That I have come this far
From a desolate place so darkened
Unconscious decisions leave scars
I see the clearing through my
water-filled eyes in tears
Higher power overcomes me
Releasing all my fears
Captivating
What a vision
Upon this peak I see
Knowing this prized possession
Was meant especially for me
What a road I have travelled
So many things I've seen
It was a hard, rugged climb
But well worth the journey

The Rest

I start my day on bended knee
All praises he is due
He gives me life and keeps me
safe
I always make it through
The troubled times
He is the shine
When darkness falls on you
He's always there
He truly cares
No matter what they do
He is the one
To surely call
With questions overdue
Never behind
Always on time
The answer's all so true
So never stray away from God
He gave us tools to use
It is the Law

For with just cause
The rest is up to you

The Land of Disbelief

In the land of disbelief
Please be careful of what you say
For the tongue in which you speak
Holds you accountable here today
Although short-lived
The lies you tell
May seem fortunes are do
But there's no pot of gold to be
found
The joke's only on you
If you talk the talk
Best walk the walk
There will be no in-between
For in the land of disbelief
All things aren't what they seem
So shield your soul with words of
truth
Honesty will be your guide
The light that shines will never
dim

So hold your head up high
In the land of disbelief
There is but one forbidden fruit
Think twice before you speak
Or let judgement pass by you

Soft Whispers

Soft whispers from heaven been
calling my name
Dodging raindrops on pillows
The storm clears once again
You are my blanket of protection
The pill that soothes all my pain
What a sight for sore eyes
To gaze upon you again
When I am awaken to the morn
Can't wait for sleep come my way
Hoping where we last left off
Is where we start the next day
I yearn the moisture from your
nurture
Before my leaves wilt away
I need the Son to strengthen me
Please ask the clouds to part the
way
What such glory it must be
To stand with He face to face
How you felt from his first hug

With you I felt the same way
The way I walk is thanks to you
A debt in whole I could not pay
If I were standing next to you
I'd try my best to find a way
Mother dear I honor you
Sweet memories won't fade away
So I know they come from you
When soft whispers from Heaven
Call my name

The Truth

Believe half of what you see
None of what you hear
Choose very careful
What you take in ear
Friends tell lies
And lies tell friends
They lie once a day
And twice on weekends
Words of wisdom are hard to find
The truth stays hidden
Behind a very thin line
And the lies you can find on the
other side
Gives truth better places he can
hide

Just open your mind
And set your conscience free
You'll find it's much easier to tell
the truth
Than it seems

Doing circles and back pedals
Are much too hard
Trying to cover up lies
Growing further from God
Telling one lie for two
Two lies for three
Before you know
That little white lie spreads like a
disease
Now the ones you love
Find it hard to believe
The words you say
You find them hare to believe

Shy of Perfect

Several days shy of perfect
Like a bird without wings
Several days shy of perfect
Like a guitar with two strings
Several days shy of perfect
Like the summer with no breeze
Several days shy of perfect
Like a tree with no leaves
Several days shy of perfect
Like the night sky without stars
Nothing lasts forever
So life's not perfect by far
Never miss for today putting off
for tomorrow
Did that a lot as a child
The only reward was sorrow
Several days shy of perfect
Like a book without words
Reading from blank pages
But wanting your voice to be
heard

Feet in the sand hiding your
hands
Throwing rocks with a curve
Feeding babies from wine glasses
Shaking hands with death
Several days shy of perfect
Like breathing your last breathe

Destiny

As I gaze upon
Afar and beyond
At the end of winters day
A limitless sky
Without sun or moon
Just the gloom of clouds at play
The open window
For angles to see
And for guardians to peer
A place for me
Serenity
Perfect for mind to clear
Though bitter cold
A gentle breeze
Caresses and warms my soul
And softly whispers
In my ear
That I am not alone
Above the trees
And mountain tops
A place for all to seek

The truth
Of which road to take
To reach your destiny

Farewell

Now the world is the biggest beast
I have seen
And it will eat you alive if you let
it.
So many people love it for the
things it posses
But that's not the way God
intended.
Walking narrow paths and
winding roads
With no sense of where they're
going.
Their lips sing a song for who they
Love
But their actions never show it.
Born by destruction, raised in the
storm,
So many times I have said
farewell.
To family, friends, and next of kin
One of life's stories to surely tell.
So I bid farewell to you, my

friend,
Just take him by the hand.
This world, you see, is small compared
To what the Lord has planned.

Hiding Places

Behind bars
Or behind scars
There is without difference
between
Both seem to be good hiding
places
Like closets and stair cases
Like rooftops
And crawlspaces
Away from home like far places
Like closed mouths
To hide lies
Or shut eyes
To hide cries
Maybe the bottom of my shoe
Is a safe place
To hide too
See I used to hide money there,
But to the contraire
Some use their hearts to hide fear.
Any dark space

Without the presence of light
Will be a great place to keep
things
Out of sight
A hat for the head
Or make-up for true beauty
But if you hide behind the truth
It won't take long to see through.

Blue Bird

As I slowly tip-toe
The blue bird flies of in a race
Like he was startled by me
Or late to be some place
Leaving his perch in the window
Now things seem out of place
Maybe it's just for the moment
Before he returns the next day
We find the essence of life
Especially when we're alone
The things we once didn't notice
Becomes and everyday norm
Like that small crack in the
window
Or that little chip in the paint
Maybe it's the little twinkle in
your eye
When I haven't seen you in a few
days
Maybe it's the question, "I wonder
why?"

After your passing away
That opens our eyes to all the
words you use to say
Why can't we all hug and hold
hands here today?
And trade our, I love you's,
before it's too late
Time waits for no one I often
heard one say
If we could turn the hands back
Would we never be late?
For if we turn the hands forward
The blue bird still flies away
Nor knowing if we'll be there to
see him in the window
The next day

Love, Faith, Family, Joy

Love, Faith, Family, Joy
The essence of life to me
Nothing else matters more
As far as I can see
In you a light shines constantly
Forever and a day
Your glow illuminates the room
You are special in every way
I thank the Lord because of you
My life is filled with JOY
You give the gift of FAMILY
I search for LOVE no more
Holding on my FAITH is strong
To my heart you hold the key
LOVE FAITH FAMILY JOY
The essence of life to me

Another Spin

Darkness roams the distance
As far as I can see
Consuming all that's in its path
But fear never becomes of me
Armed with the inhibitions
Received by pedigree
Intriguing footprints left in
struggle
Amongst a dying breed
I walk a winding road
A mystery at every turn
With every lesson bought
There lies a lesson learned
Winter nights without a coat
Frozen sweat to hide the shivers
Forbidden fruit seduce my soul
Make my camp east of the river
With two voices fighting words in
ear
My restitutions due
State property I paid in full,

By days in solitude
A game with many players
But very few to win
I would rather shoot the dice
Than to take another spin

Mr. Squirrel

Over the roof down the gutter
into the white oak tree
Mr. Squirrel quickly passes by me
On the daily hunt for acorns,
pecans, any nut
He can find to make his dinner
complete
On the hunt, stay away from Mr.
Hawk who preys on Mr. Squirrel
For his dinner today
In the cool month of November
Hope he makes it till December
And give thanks for the smooth
get-a-way

The Gift

No gift so great in the eyes of the
Lord
Just seek and ye shall find
From the food that we eat to the
air that we breathe
It is from He the true divine
Every step that we take
Every move that we make
All praises He is due
In the mirror you will find
There's one above the rest
The biggest gift from He is you

Hold Strong

Above the trees
Amongst thieves
In the shallows of inhibition
Making promises
Breaking promises
In retrospect from not listening
So many ways
I could have made
A better bed for me to lay in
I chose the way
Over the hill
Under the fence and through the
ditches
In the dark
When no one's looking
I always said they couldn't see
I'm so thankful
That God was watching
They couldn't get the best of me
Not a lake

Could hold the tears
River nor the sea
I found the way
Rely on faith
And hold strong on bended knee

Through the Storm

I love the rain
Why would I shelter
Away from the tears of thee
Knowing solely
I am sinner
He shed first his tears for me
When it's snowing
No need for a coat
For the truth it blankets me
With a naked soul
He provided clothes
Gave me the Spirit to help me
breathe
Bare footed, a rocky path
He positioned shoes
Upon my feet
Without sight
He provided light
No need for glasses, now I can see
Homeless I roamed
Through alley ways

But now I have a place to stay
You can run
But you can't dodge rain drops
Through the storm is the only way

Guardian Angel

As I toss and turn on sheets of
cotton
At last the night and day's
forgotten
The boom of struggle from wince
I came
Is gently settled by drops of rain
Upon my window seal so clear
I squeeze my pillow like my dear
Now soon I drift amongst the
dream
Engage my mind on pleasant
things
So soft a nest prepared for me
Underneath moons silhouette I
sleep
Said goodnight to God a vow to
keep
Then lose my count among the
sheep
A whistle comes from the twilight
breeze

Such a soothing song like the
song bird sings
A smile secures he's there for me
A true guardian angel and that is
He

Acknowledgments

Ever since I can remember, I have always been inspired to write. It would be without just cause if I didn't acknowledge those great people for whom I am truly indebted. In particular-for providing the essential tools, support, and the encouragement for me to make a change in my life.

So I wish to extend special gratitude to:
JD and Erma Jean white (my parents), Monica Sloane, Jerry White Sr., Veronica White, Frederick White, Andrea White, Rosie White, Margaret White (my wife), Theodore Seuss Getsel (The Cat in the Hat), Judy Blume (Tales of a fourth grade nothing), Maya Angelo (I Know Why The Caged Bird Sings), Edgar Alan Poe (The Raven), and the Dee Brown Library at 6325 Baseline road for providing a place of tranquility for me to study and write my manuscripts.

"I have learned people will forget what you said, people will forget what you did, but people will never forget how you made them feel."

-Maya Angelou

"Yesterday is history,
Tomorrow is a mystery,
But today is a blessing from God."

J. Kenkade
PUBLISHING®

Also Available from J. Kenkade Publishing

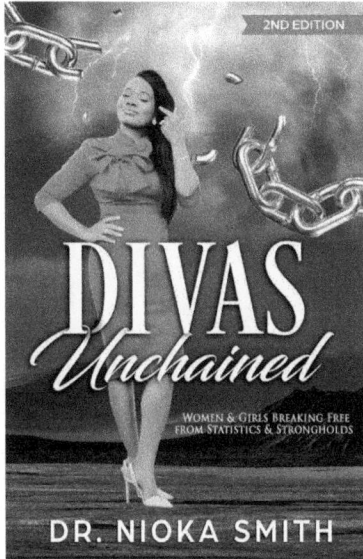

ISBN: 978-1-944486-25-9
Visit www.drniokasmith.com
Author: Dr. Nioka Smith

Sexually abused by her father at the age of 14, pregnant at the age of 17, and a nervous breakdown at the age of 28, Dr. Nioka Smith's painful past almost killed her, until the voice of the Lord guided her into destroying strongholds and reversing Satan's plan for her life. DIVAS Unchained is the powerful chain-breaking reality of the many unfortunate strongholds our women and girls face. Dr. Nioka uses her divine gift to help women and girls break free from destructive life cycles and prosper in all areas of life. Satan has lied to you. It's time to expose his lies. It's time to break free!

Also Available from
J. Kenkade Publishing

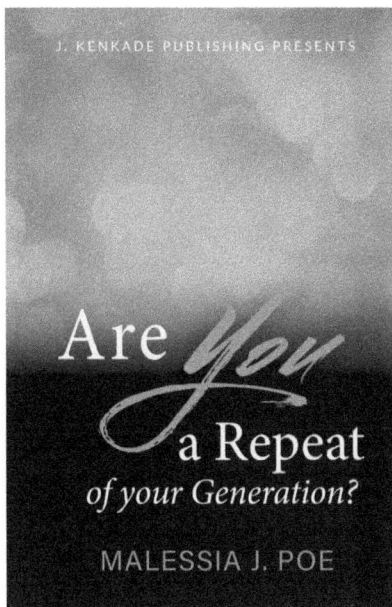

ISBN: 978-1-944486-36-5
Visit www.jkenkadepublishing.com
Author: Malessia J. Poe

Have you been sabotaged?
Are you the victim of a generational curse?
Have you ever wondered, "Why am I here? Why do cycles repeat themselves in my life?" There is a hidden assassination attempt on your life by the enemy. However, God is a concerned God who wants to bring us into the full development and knowledge of who we are. God wants us to stand steadfast in the liberty he has given us and root our identities in Him. It's time to move forward and break the cycle!

Also Available from J. Kenkade Publishing

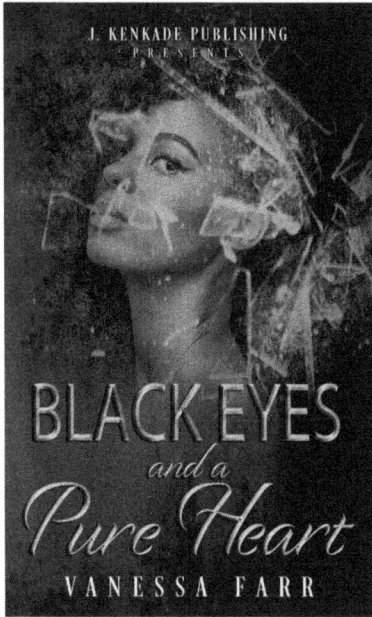

ISBN: 978-1-944486-23-5
Visit www.jkenkadepublishing.com
Author: Vanessa Farr

Black Eyes and a Pure Heart is a novel about the life of a young girl who must figure out how to live her life with a child at the age of 17. When the baby is born, her supportive spouse becomes an abusive predator. The black eyes represent the malicious nature of the domestic violence in the face of evil that so desperately tried to kill her. This short story reveals that the wrong path in life can gravely disfigure and blacken the eyes of young women and girls who seek easy pleasure.

Also Available from
J. Kenkade Publishing

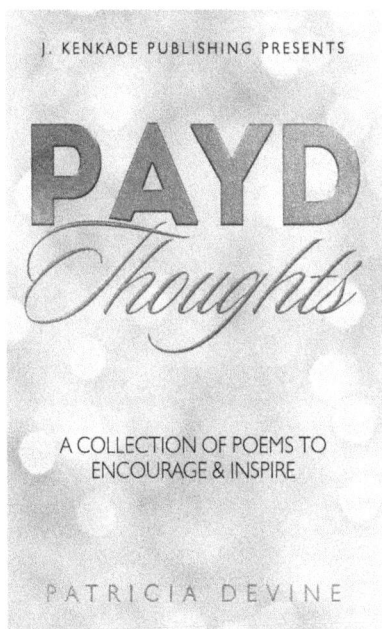

J. KENKADE PUBLISHING PRESENTS

PAYD
Thoughts

A COLLECTION OF POEMS TO
ENCOURAGE & INSPIRE

PATRICIA DEVINE

ISBN: 978-1-944486-18-1
Visit www.jkenkadepublishing.com
Author: Patricia Devine

"PAYD Thoughts" is a collection of poems that focus on various subjects inspired by Patricia's experiences shared with the hope of encouraging and inspiring readers in similar situations. "PAYD Thoughts" discusses race relations, love towards God, unhealthy relationships, and depression.

www.ingramcontent.com/pod-product-compliance
Lightning Source LLC
Chambersburg PA
CBHW051841040426
42447CB00006B/634